Pope, showing the Pope's support for his claim to the throne. William also claimed that Harold Godwinson had sworn an **oath** of loyalty to him in 1064, and therefore supported his claim. Much confusion surrounds this event. It seems that Harold had been shipwrecked off the French coast, and was taken prisoner by William. Harold later claimed that his oath of loyalty to William was invalid, as he had only sworn it to gain his freedom.

Harald Hardrada

Harald Hardrada (meaning 'hard ruler') was a powerful Viking King of Norway, who had fought across Europe and Asia. He vowed to add England to his Scandinavian Empire, claiming that England still belonged to the Vikings as it had during the days of King Canute.

Hardrada had a very useful ally: Harold Godwinson's hot-headed younger brother Tostig. Harold and Tostig had fallen out bitterly in 1065 when Harold stripped his brother of his earldom in Northumbria for being a bad ruler, and sent him into **exile**. Tostig was now willing to betray his brother and fight for Hardrada's Vikings.

Fact

Once, when the Duke of Normandy was laying siege to Alençon Castle in France, the inhabitants taunted him about his mother's lowly status. Having taken the castle, William had his revenge by cutting off the hands and feet of every inhabitant.

Battle of Stamford Bridge

In September, King Harold's army was stationed in the south of England preparing for an invasion from the **Normans**. However, he received the shocking news that Hardrada and Tostig had invaded England's north-east coast, and taken control of the old Viking capital, York. Harold marched his army north to meet the Vikings, covering 180 miles in just four days.

This caught the Viking army completely by surprise, and the two armies met at a location called Stamford Bridge on 25 September. Many Vikings did not even have time to put on their armour, and Harold's army destroyed them, killing both Hardrada and Tostig. Of an invasion fleet of around 300 ships, fewer than 30 ships were needed to take what remained of the Viking army back to Norway.

According to a Saxon legend, a great Viking fighter held off the English attack on the bridge, so that they could not finish off the retreating Viking army. Nobody could kill this fearsome Viking, until an English soldier had the clever idea of floating under the bridge and thrusting his spear into the Viking's foot.

Stamford Bridge in Yorkshire, the site of the battle today, where an 18th-century bridge now stands

Check your understanding

1. Why was the death of Edward the Confessor met with such confusion?
2. What was Harold Godwinson's claim to the English throne?
3. What was William of Normandy's claim to the English throne?
4. What was Harald Hardrada's claim to the English throne?
5. How did Harold Godwinson defeat Hardrada's Viking army?

The Battle of Hastings

Harold's victory at Stamford Bridge was an astonishing success. However, while Harold's army was celebrating, a messenger arrived with dreadful news from the south.

On 28 September, just 3 days after the Battle of Stamford Bridge, William, Duke of Normandy had landed on the south-east coast of England with his invasion force.

Since August, William had been camped on the French coast ready to invade, but the winds had not been in his favour, and by the end of September it seemed he had missed his chance. Harold even called in his navy, which had been guarding the English Channel, thinking that a Norman invasion would be delayed until the following year. But all of a sudden the winds changed and William was able to sail across the Channel unchallenged.

Ruins of Battle Abbey. The abbey was built by William the Conqueror on the site of the Battle of Hastings.

William's Norman army numbered 10 000 men, with 3000 heavily armoured Norman **knights** on horseback: the tanks of medieval Europe. As William stepped off his boat, he tripped and fell on the beach. His troops looked worried at this bad omen, but as he rose William picked up two fists full of sand and declared "Look how easily I take this land!"

Harold's army marches south

The Norman army marched 10 miles inland to Hastings, where they quickly built a wooden castle, and prepared for Harold to attack. With wounds still fresh from battle, Harold's army began a 200-mile trek from Stamford Bridge to the south coast. They stopped in London, where many of Harold's advisers begged him to rest and rebuild his forces before attacking the Norman army. However, Harold wanted to surprise William just as he had surprised Hardrada's Viking army. After a week gaining reinforcements, Harold resumed his march south.

At 9 a.m. on 14 October, the two armies met 10 miles outside Hastings. Harold had left many of his best soldiers in the north, but kept the core of his army: 3000 fearsome **huscarls** – the King's professional soldiers and bodyguard. The rest of the army consisted of the fyrd, around 5000 part-time soldiers, some armed with little more than a pike.

Fact

The **Bayeux Tapestry** is 70 metres long, and tells the entire story of William of Normandy's **conquest** of England. It is one of medieval Europe's most important artefacts. Bishop Odo, William's half-brother, commissioned the tapestry during the 1070s as a gift to his brother.

Extract from the Bayeux Tapestry

The battle

Arriving at the battlefield, Harold's army took the high ground on top of Senlac Hill, and formed a long defensive 'shield wall' of troops chanting 'ut, ut!' ('out, out!').

This was an excellent start for the Saxons: the Norman knights could not break through the wall as their horses lost speed galloping uphill, and the Norman archers were ineffective when they fired their arrows upwards. Harold's army stood its ground, taking great swings at the Norman knights with their axes. At one point, a rumour spread across the battlefield that William, Duke of Normandy was dead. But then William removed his helmet and called out to his troops that he was still alive.

Modern illustration of the death of King Harold

After hours of struggling to break through the Saxon shield wall, the Normans called a retreat. Harold's army was overjoyed and broke out of their formation to chase and kill off the retreating Norman soldiers. However, the retreat had been a trick: William ordered it to tempt the Saxon soldiers away from the high ground and to break their shield wall. The Normans now regrouped, and picked off the disorganised Saxon soldiers. King Harold was killed, but to this day there is no agreement about how this happened (see box).

Without their king, most of the Saxon soldiers fled the battlefield, but Harold's huscarls – who were sworn to protect the king – fought to the death. The brutal battle lasted 6 hours and William was victorious. Having defeated Harold's army, William could spread his power throughout England. William, Duke of Normandy was now 'William the Conqueror', and the history of England had been changed forever.

The death of King Harold

There remains much disagreement among historians over how Harold died. The first account of the battle, written by the Bishop of Amiens, states that four knights were sent to find Harold on the battlefield and kill him. One knight knocked him to the floor, while two others beheaded and **disembowelled** the Saxon king.

However, in later accounts Harold was said to have been struck in the eye with an arrow, and this is what the Bayeux tapestry appears to show beneath the words 'Harold Rex Interfectus Est' (King Harold is killed).

Check your understanding

1. What stroke of luck did William, Duke of Normandy enjoy at the end of September?
2. Why did Harold Godwinson hurry into fighting the Norman army?
3. Who had the stronger army at the start of the Battle of Hastings: the Normans or the Saxons?
4. How did the Norman army's false retreat give them the chance to win the battle?
5. What story does the Bayeux Tapestry tell?

The Norman Conquest

On Christmas Day 1066, 2 months after he defeated Harold, William was crowned King William I of England at Westminster Abbey.

The Norman knights guarding the coronation were fearful of a popular rebellion, and mistook cheers from inside the Abbey as a revolt. In response, they burnt the surrounding houses, and killed any Englishmen too slow to flee. It was a violent beginning to a violent reign.

Following his victory against King Harold at Hastings, William's approach to conquering England was brutally effective. Wherever resistance or rebellion occurred, his heavily armoured knights descended on the Anglo-Saxon communities, burning down villages and slaughtering the inhabitants. Within a few years, England's two million Anglo-Saxons inhabitants were living under the military occupation of just 20 000 Norman invaders.

Silver English penny of William the Conqueror

Norman nobles

Before invading England, William promised the Norman knights who fought for him that they would be richly rewarded with English land. The Anglo-Saxon noblemen, many of whom died on the battlefield at Hastings, had their land seized from their families and given to Norman knights. William established a **royal court** consisting of French noblemen, and a new ruling class with French names, such as Beaufort, Neville and Sinclair, spread across the country.

Wherever they were granted land, Norman nobles built large defensive structures with a French name: 'castle'. At first, these were simple '**motte-and-bailey castles**' which were quick and easy to build: a ditch would be dug and the earth would create an artificial hill, on top of which a wooden tower would be built. Gradually, these were replaced with stronger, stone castles – stern buildings which symbolised a foreign, occupying force.

The Harrying of the North

Many Anglo-Saxons rebelled against Norman rule. In the north-east of England, the local population twice rose up against their new **lords**. On the second occasion in 1069, the northern rebels took Durham Castle, murdered its Norman earl, Robert de Commines, and slaughtered most of his garrison. The rebels then took York and proclaimed Edward the Confessor's Anglo-Saxon nephew, Edgar the Ætheling, to be the rightful King of England.

William was furious. He vowed to make an example of the northern rebels. His army marched north, and burnt to the ground every village between York and Durham. Farm animals were slaughtered, crops were destroyed, and the fields were laced with salt so that no more food could be grown. Much of the population was killed, and whole areas of the north-east became uninhabited wastelands. One estimate suggested 100 000 people starved to death, and while this was probably an exaggeration, England's north-east remained sparsely populated for centuries to come.

The Harrying of the North showed William the Conqueror at his most ruthless. The Norman chronicler Orderic Vitalis wrote, "I have often praised William before, but I cannot for this act, which caused both the innocent and the guilty alike to die by slow starvation... Such brutal slaughter cannot go unpunished".

Modern illustration of the Harrying of the North

Hereward the Wake

The east of England had long been a stronghold of Anglo-Saxon power, and it was here the final rebellion against Norman rule occurred in 1070. The land surrounding a town called Ely was made up of marshes and rivers, and often covered in mist. Here, an Anglo-Saxon noble named Hereward the Wake and his band of outlaws would ambush Norman knights, kill them, and disappear into the mist.

Hereward's stand against the Normans came to an end when William arrived outside Ely, and built a 2-mile wooden causeway across the marshes. Norman knights rode into the town, and the Saxon rebels were killed, imprisoned, blinded or had their arms chopped off. Hereward escaped, and some claimed that William had spared his life on purpose as he admired his bravery.

Hereward's heroic deeds, along with his sword known as 'Brainbiter', quickly passed into popular legend, but such stories were a small comfort for Saxons living under Norman rule.

Norman rule

Few Anglo-Saxon nobles survived William's invasion, and those that did were forced to swear an oath of loyalty to their new king. A favourite trick of William's was to demand a noble's son as a hostage, to make sure that the noble stayed loyal. At first, William suggested that he might learn English, but soon it became clear he would not. French became the language of government, business and the royal court, and England entered a new era under the rule of William and his Norman descendents.

> ### Fact
> After the Norman Conquest, many French words entered the English language, such as castle, battle, punishment, judge, colour and fruit.

Check your understanding

1. Why did William the Conqueror's coronation end in violence?
2. What happened to the land belonging to England's Anglo-Saxon noblemen?
3. What did William the Conqueror do to punish the rebels who rose up against him in the north-east?
4. How did William the Conqueror finally defeat Hereward the Wake?
5. What was one of the tactics William used to ensure loyalty from the Anglo-Saxon nobility?

The feudal system

Under the control of William and his Norman knights, English society was transformed, and a rigid social structure developed.

The higher up you were, the more land, wealth and power you held. The lower down you were, the poorer and less free you became.

English society had a clear **hierarchy**, shaped like a pyramid: the few at the top were the strongest, and the many at the bottom were the weakest, owing their duty and service to those above them. Anyone below you was your '**vassal**', and anyone above you was your 'lord'. This social structure was called the **feudal system**.

The king

Right at the top of the feudal system was the king. It was believed that the king was appointed by God, and only those with royal blood, who were descended from William the Conqueror, could sit on the throne. The king was answerable only to God, and all who lived in his kingdom were his **subjects**. However, the king still needed loyal friends to rule different parts of his kingdom on his behalf.

Illustration of King William I

The barons

For this reason, the king granted land to his **barons**, around 200 of the most powerful knights in the country. In return for their land, the king's barons had to pay homage to him and swear an oath of **fealty**. This meant that if ever there was a war, the barons had to fight on behalf of their king. In the centre of their vast stretches of land, barons built fortified castles to keep them safe from enemy attacks. Some had the noble title of 'Earl', and their titles and lands were **hereditary**, meaning that they passed down from the father to his eldest son.

At the same level of power as the barons were the **bishops** and archbishops of the medieval Church. The church was extremely powerful, and owned much of England's land. Its bishops enjoyed huge wealth and influence and were part of the ruling class.

The knights

In order to fight for their king, barons needed their own armies. So, they divided their own land into smaller areas led by their knights. Each baron had around 20 knights. A knight would swear an oath of fealty to his baron, and gain a number of manor houses or smaller castles in return.

The peasants

Below the knights were the **peasants**, who made up the great majority of medieval society. Many were bound to work the land of their lord until the day they died. Some peasants were not allowed to marry or leave

Illustration of a Norman Knight

home without their lord's permission. A lord would grant his peasants a small area of land to farm, and they had to work his land in return. The difference between a kind and a cruel lord could mean the difference between happiness and misery for a medieval vassal.

The Domesday book

Two years before he died, William the Conqueror ordered that a survey should be written detailing the possessions of every single settlement in England. As king, William wanted to know precisely what this new country of his contained. Once he knew what the English people owned, he could tax them accordingly to pay for his armies and castles.

For 2 years, Norman commissioners were sent the length and breadth of England, with the order that not a single cow nor pig should escape their notice. They visited 13 418 different towns and villages, and wrote down two million words. The official name of the record was 'The King's Roll', but it became more commonly known as the '**Domesday Book**'.

'Doomsday' is another name for the Day of Judgment, when Christians believe that Jesus Christ will return to the earth and pass judgment on both the living and the dead. The Anglo-Saxons chose this nickname with a sarcastic sense of humour, as they disliked a foreign king forcing them to declare everything they owned so that he could pass judgment on them.

Today, the Domesday Book provides us with a fascinating picture of what England was like at the end of the 11th century, right down to the last fishpond and beehive. We hear the nicknames of English peasants, such as Alwin the Rat and Ralph the Haunted. In 1085, Birmingham, which is England's second largest city today, was a small village with just nine families, and two ploughs.

Modern illustration of the writing of the Domesday book

Fact

Over 70 English forests became Royal hunting grounds. If a peasant was found hunting there, he could be punished by blinding or mutilation. Some peasants were even made to wear deer skin and be hunted themselves!

Check your understanding

1. What was the shape of medieval English society?
2. In return for being granted land, what did barons do for the king?
3. What powers did a medieval lord have over the peasants who worked his land?
4. Why did William the Conqueror commission the Domesday Book to be written?
5. How did the Domesday Book earn its nickname?

The Norman monarchs

Towards the end of his life, William the Conqueror grew very fat, but this did not stop him from going on military campaigns.

In 1087, while laying siege to the town of Mantes in northern France, William's horse stood on some hot stones and reared up. The king was impaled on the pommel of his saddle, and he died 6 weeks later.

As seemed to be the tradition for Norman Kings, William did not get on well with each of his three sons. He ruled an empire stretching across England and Normandy, and by right, all his land should have passed to his eldest son Robert. However, William disliked Robert – he even nicknamed him 'Curthose' or 'stubby legs'. So, William gave Normandy to his eldest son Robert, England to his middle son William, and £5000 to his youngest son Henry. This would prove to be a grave mistake.

William, Rufus and Henry I

William II was an unpleasant king. Nicknamed 'Rufus' for his red hair, he was angry and short-tempered, and offended the church through his open disdain for religion. On a summer's day in August 1100, William was hunting in the New Forest with his close friend Walter Tirel. Tirel was known for being a good archer, but when shooting at a stag, he missed and hit William II straight in the chest. The king dropped to the floor and died instantly. Tirel fled the scene, travelling to France where he died later that year in exile.

William's younger brother Henry, who was also at the hunt, acted quickly. On hearing the news of his brother's death he rode to Winchester and 3 days later was crowned Henry I. For centuries, historians have wondered whether the death of William II was an accident, or a deliberate plot.

In 1106, Henry I captured his eldest brother Robert on the battlefield in Normandy. He seized Robert's French land and imprisoned him in Cardiff Castle for the last 30 years of his life. Through imprisoning one older brother and (perhaps) killing another, in just 6 years the youngest son of William the Conqueror had gone from ruling nothing, to ruling over the whole of his father's empire. Henry I ruled England for 35 peaceful years.

Henry I married a princess named Matilda, who was descended from the Anglo-Saxon House of Wessex. Together, they had one son named William but he died on board the White Ship in 1120 (see box).

> ### Fact
> Having grown fat in his old age, William was too large for his stone coffin at his funeral. When the attendants tried to force his body inside the coffin his body burst. The mourners fled as a putrid smell spread through the church.

Modern illustration of the sinking of the White Ship

The White Ship

On a cold November evening, Henry I and his 17-year-old son William were due to sail for England from the Norman port of Barfleur. Henry I left early, but William and his friends chose to stay behind getting drunk and finally left around midnight. The young men were on a newly built vessel named the White Ship, and they challenged their crew to overtake the king's ship.

The White Ship's crew had also been drinking. As the vessel left the port, it struck a rock off the Normandy coast. The boat sank, killing Henry I's only son and **heir**, along with many other **Anglo-Norman** nobles.

The Anarchy

With no son as heir, Henry I's death in 1135 threw England into conflict. Two cousins both claimed the throne: Henry's daughter the Empress Matilda, who had been married to a German Emperor, and Henry's nephew Stephen. Stephen was a friendly, well-liked figure among the Anglo-Norman nobility, whereas Empress Matilda was seen as distant and arrogant. More importantly, few Norman lords were prepared to be ruled by a woman. While Matilda was in France, Stephen was crowned King of England in December 1135.

Stephen and Matilda's rival claims threw England into a 19-year **civil war**, in which law and order completely broke down. Great areas of the country had no royal authority, leaving the people at the mercy of cruel barons, who used the civil war as an excuse to terrorise their vassals. For this reason, the period is remembered as 'The **Anarchy**'. The Anglo-Saxon Chronicle gives a vivid account of these dreadful years, describing people being forced into labour, imprisoned and tortured. It ends: "To till the ground was to plough the sea; the earth bare no corn, for the lands were all laid waste by such deeds; and men said openly that Christ and his saints were asleep."

14th-century illustration of Empress Matilda

Check your understanding

1. How did William the Conqueror split his empire between his three sons when he died?

2. What were the suspicious circumstances surrounding William II's death?

3. Which of William the Conqueror's three sons eventually ended up ruling England?

4. Why did the sinking of the White Ship in 1120 throw England into a state of confusion?

5. Why was the civil war between Stephen and Matilda so unpleasant for the English population?

Knowledge organiser

1051 Edward the Confessor promises the English throne to William, Duke of Normandy

1066 (Oct) The Battle of Hastings

1064 Harold Godwinson swears an oath of loyalty to William, Duke of Normandy

1066 (Sep) The Battle of Stamford Bridge

1066 (Dec) William I crowned King of England

Key vocabulary

Anarchy A state of disorder caused by a lack of law or authority

Anglo-Norman The ruling class in England after 1066, composed of Normans who had settled in England

Baron The highest rank of medieval society, ruling land directly on behalf of the king

Bayeux Tapestry A 70-metre long embroidered cloth depicting William of Normandy's conquest of England

Bishop A Christian clergyman with authority over a large number of priests and churches

Civil war A war between two sides from the same nation

Conquest Taking control of a place or people through military force

Disembowel To cut someone open, and remove their internal organs

Domesday Book A book commissioned by William the Conqueror detailing the possessions of every settlement in England

Exile Being forced to live outside your native country, typically for political reasons

Fealty A pledge of loyalty from a feudal vassal to their lord

Feudal system The structure of medieval society, where land was exchanged for service and loyalty

Heir A person set to inherit property or a title, often used to mean next in line to the throne

Hereditary Passed through a family, from parents to their children

Hierarchy A form of social organisation where people are ranked according to status or power

Huscarls The professional bodyguard of Anglo-Saxon kings

Illegitimate Not recognised as lawful, once used to describe someone born of unmarried parents

Knight Soldiers on horseback who belonged to the nobility

Lord A general term for a medieval landholder, or a member of the peerage today

Monarch A royal head of state, can be a king, queen or emperor

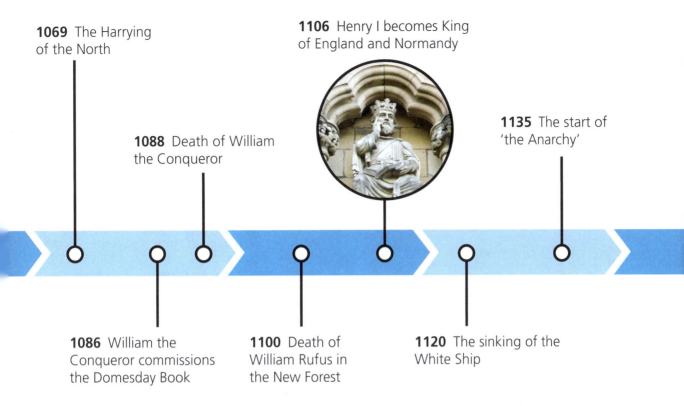

1069 The Harrying of the North

1106 Henry I becomes King of England and Normandy

1088 Death of William the Conqueror

1135 The start of 'the Anarchy'

1086 William the Conqueror commissions the Domesday Book

1100 Death of William Rufus in the New Forest

1120 The sinking of the White Ship

Key vocabulary

Motte-and-bailey castle A simple fortification with an artificial hill and a defensive courtyard

Noble Member of the nobility, with land and titles that passes through the generations

Normans People from a region in northern France, who were descended from Viking invaders

Oath A solemn promise, often said to be witnessed by God

Omen An event that is thought to foretell the future, perhaps as a message from the Gods

Peasant The lowest member of medieval society, usually a farm labourer

Royal blood Possessed by those who are blood relatives of a ruling monarch

Royal court A collection of nobles and clergymen, known as courtiers, who advise the monarch

Subject A member of a country or territory under the rule of a monarch

Vassal Anyone who was below you in medieval society, and had to call you 'my lord'

Key people

Edward the Confessor An Anglo-Saxon King of England whose death triggered the Norman invasion

Empress Matilda The daughter of Henry I, who fought for the English throne during 'The Anarchy'

Harald Hardrada A fierce Viking warrior, who made a claim for the English throne in 1066

Harold Godwinson The last Anglo-Saxon King of England, who led the Saxons at the Battle of Hastings

Henry I The youngest son of William the Conqueror who became King after the death of his brother William II

Hereward the Wake A legendary Saxon rebel who held out against the Norman invaders in Ely

William, Duke of Normandy A French duke who conquered England in 1066

William II The middle son of William the Conqueror, he was nicknamed 'Rufus' due to his red hair

Quiz questions

Chapter 1: Saxon, Norman or Viking?

1. Which Anglo-Saxon king died in 1066 with no clear heir?
2. Which Anglo-Saxon earl was crowned following the death of the king?
3. This claimant to the throne was Earl of what area of England?
4. William was Duke of what area in northern France?
5. What did William say happened in 1051, which lay at the root of his claim?
6. Who sent a banner to William showing support for his cause?
7. Which Viking king of Norway also claimed the English throne?
8. Who betrayed Harold Godwinson by joining the Vikings?
9. For how long did the Anglo-Saxon army march to meet the Vikings, once they had invaded north east England?
10. At what battle did the Anglo-Saxons defeat the Vikings in September 1066?

Chapter 2: The Battle of Hastings

1. In what month and year did the Battle of Hastings take place?
2. What suddenly changed at the end of September, allowing William's Norman army to invade?
3. What were William's heavily armoured soldiers on horseback called?
4. What were Harold's force of 3 000 professional soldiers and bodyguard called?
5. What 70-metre-long embroidered cloth depicted the Norman Conquest of England?
6. On top of what did Harold's army position themselves at the start of the battle?
7. What did Harold's army form, which the Normans found difficult to break through?
8. What did the Normans carry out, to tempt the Saxons away from their high ground?
9. How did Harold Godwinson die, according to the Bayeux Tapestry?
10. How did Harold Godwinson die according to the first account of the battle?

Chapter 3: The Norman Conquest

1. When was William the Conqueror crowned King of England?
2. Where was William the Conqueror crowned King of England?
3. What type of castles did Norman nobles first build on their newly acquired English land?
4. What collection of nobles and clergymen would advise the king?
5. What event took place in 1069, following an Anglo-Saxon rebellion in Durham?
6. How many people are claimed to have starved to death following this event?
7. Which Anglo-Saxon noble led a last stand against Norman power in East Anglia?
8. In what town did he base his rebellion?
9. According to legend, what was the name of his sword?
10. What did William force all surviving Anglo-Saxon nobles to do?

Chapter 4: The feudal system

1. What form of social organisation ranks people according to status or power?
2. What did you call anyone below you in the feudal system?
3. Which rank came just below the king in the feudal system, and ruled land on his behalf?
4. Roughly how many people of this rank existed in medieval England?
5. What did this rank of people have to do for the king, in return for being granted land?
6. What term describes a title that is passed through a family, from parents to their children?
7. What pledge of loyalty would a vassal have to swear to their lord?
8. What rank, usually a farm labourer, was at the bottom of medieval society?
9. What vitally important book did William the Conqueror commission in 1086?
10. For what primary purpose did William the Conqueror have this book written?

Chapter 5: The Norman monarchs

1. Who became King of England after the death of William the Conqueror in 1088?
2. Where did this king die?
3. Who killed him with a stray arrow?
4. Who became King of England from 1100 to 1135?
5. Which of his brothers did the new King of England defeat and imprison in 1106?
6. What area of land, formerly ruled by his father, did victory in 1106 give him?
7. What boat sank in 1120, killing the king's heir and many Anglo-Norman nobles?
8. Who became King of England in 1135?
9. Who also claimed the throne, leading to a 19-year civil war?
10. What name is used to describe the lawlessness and disorder of this civil war?